UNFOLLOW ME

YOUR GUIDE FOR FINANCIAL DISCIPLINE

ADITYA

notionpress.com

INDIA • SINGAPORE • MALAYSIA

Notion Press

Old No. 38, New No. 6
McNichols Road, Chetpet
Chennai - 600 031

First Published by Notion Press 2018
Copyright © Aditya 2018
All Rights Reserved.

ISBN 978-1-64429-583-0

Blessed by God

&

Gurus

CONTENTS

ACKNOWLEDGEMENTS

With high regards and the deepest gratitude, I would like to thank all those who touched my life and played an important role in shaping me.

While writing the book, my well wishers Ravi, Audi, Srini, Kingshuk, Megha, and Uday have given me their valuable feedback. It has helped me immensely. Dr. Ch. Srinivas, my friend, philosopher, and guide, has been with me throughout the process.

Rishi Puri helped me with a few tips about social media and publishing. My neighbour, Ravi Shankar (SAMURA), has helped me in contacting Notion Press.

I would also thank all the employees at Notion Press for their support and valuable inputs. I thank the editors, designers, Rashmi, Arun, and all those people who helped me with the process.

I also want to thank my friends Sunil Chakravarthy, Sanjay, Anil R, Anil Nayyar, Sunil Patel, Pradhyuman, Deepak, Rakesh, Vishal, Prashanth, and Dr. Kabra. I can count on their support at any point in my life.

I'm nothing without the love, wishes, prayers, and blessings of my family – mom, dad, mother-in-law, late father-in-law, Vissu, Rama, Harshith, Mahathi, Nagesh, Aruna, Anirudh, Uday, Geetha, Anu, Valli, and Hansini.

My wife, Lakshmi, and my son, Chakkradar, are a constant source of love, energy, and support for me. They are with me through thick and thin of my life. I learn a lot from them. My house is a home because of them.

I'm hoping that this effort of mine will help you accomplish your dreams.

STAY HAPPY AND STAY BLESSED!

1

THE NEED

Two years back, I was travelling alone and slipped into some deep thoughts. While I'm doing well in my career, I'm still a bit unsatisfied as I'm not doing what I'd love to do. And for me to do what I'd love to do, I need to be financially independent. That financial independence seemed as far away as it ever was.

When I completed my education, I had a few dreams. Along with those dreams, I also had a few financial commitments. My dreams wouldn't help me meet my commitments, well at least not immediately. It would take a few years for me to make money if I pursued my dreams. And there was a risk of failure.

So, what did I do?

I started working so it would help me with my finances and I postponed chasing my dreams for a while. The deal was to work for ten years, gain financial independence, and then work on accomplishing my dreams. My curriculum vitae now shows 18+ years of experience and guess what? The financial independence that I was seeking is farther now than before. Does it mean I am where I was a couple of decades ago?

When I look back, I have a decent career graph. Well paying jobs, sexy titles, and powerful positions. I didn't waste a lot of money on "too many" unwanted luxuries. My family spends cautiously. I live in an upscale society. Then why is it that I'm still financially dependent on a job?

I took a pen and a piece of paper and started doing the math. When I finished, I realised my mistakes. While I can be considered well off, I still don't have the money that I need to be financially independent. That's when I began listing down things to take corrective action. At the end of it, I was happy that I would be able to achieve financial independence in less than ten years. At the same time, I felt stupid because I didn't think of it before. It was neither a great secret that I uncovered nor was it rocket-science that it took me so long to figure out.

To be honest, it's very simple. Yet most of us miss the trick – in many instances, it either takes a eureka moment or a coach.

Two years after I began implementing whatever I decided, financially, I feel that I'm in a more comfortable state. Now, I'm a lot more confident of accomplishing my goal than I ever was. This is when I decided to make this knowledge available to the public.

Mind you, I'm neither saying that no one ever knew this or saying that this is based on scientific research. All I'm saying is that this is pure common sense and we often don't realise what we are doing.

In this book, I'll give you simple tips to attain your financial goals. And I'm sure you know either some or all of these. Also, while the point of reference is a salaried person, a self-employed individual too can use these tips with slight modifications. My attempt is to see that you don't fall into the common money traps like I did, and don't miss out on realising your financial goals. I want you to avoid following my path and making the mistakes I made.

I'm deliberately keeping the book short and crisp. This will help you finish reading it in a few hours and can also work as a quick reference guide whenever needed. I hope you will accomplish your dreams earlier than expected and live your dream life.

MONEY MATTERS

(To be filled in by the readers)

Financial independence is to have an adequate and a regular stream of income without having to work for it.

To secure financial independence, I need a monthly income of Rs.................. by the year ....

Securing financial independence is important for me because it will help me (list down the things that you would like to do in your life when you don't have to work for a living).

1. _______________________________________

____

____

2. _______________________________________

____

____

3. _______________________________________

____

____

2

FIRST STEP

"Don't save what's left after spending, spend what's left after saving."

— **Warren Buffett**

I started off by looking at my income and expenses. Do you remember the moment you got your first job or received an increment?

In most of the instances, I'm sure you've already spent the entire money (mentally, of course!) even before you saw it in your bank account. I don't know about you, but I surely did. Unfortunately, the fact of life is that the expenses arrive way before the income does.

While there are a lot of theories floating around about how you should invest your income, let's take a simple yet effective way to arrive at what you can invest. Remember, this should be the first thing that you do the moment your income is determined. Don't fall into the trap of committing to any expenses before you finish this exercise. Well, I recommend you avoid committing to any expenses till you finish reading this book.

Firstly, identify all the expenses that are **unavoidable**. These are the expenses that are needed for your survival. ABSOLUTELY NECESSARY! Food, rent, transport (to and from office), telephone, and stuff like that form the unavoidable expenses. While categorising an expense as unavoidable, be brutally harsh with yourself. You have to question your survival while determining if an expense is unavoidable or not.

Expenses that are needed for you to survive or expenses that provide you with basic comforts can be put here. If you feel comfortable wearing a particular brand of clothes or shoes, then they are unavoidable. Remember, the intent is not to starve you or put yourself through unnecessary hardships in life. However, liking the look of an expensive Swiss watch brand over a decent local brand that costs a fraction of that Swiss brand doesn't qualify it to be unavoidable.

The next step is to identify the **avoidable expenses**. These are the expenses that you often get tempted to spend but can be avoided. Eating out frequently when you have an opportunity to savour home-cooked delicacies is a classic example of avoidable expenses. While the intent is not to stop eating out completely, you can probably look at reducing the frequency.

Finally, identify the **money-stealers**. It often gets tricky to differentiate between **avoidable expenses** and **money-stealers**. While eating out, in my opinion, can be avoided, eating out at expensive joints or eating out frequently is nothing but throwing your money down the drain.

The idea is to identify the expenses that can be avoided. This will increase the amount that is at your disposal. Remember the old adage – ***"money saved is money earned."***

This exercise will help you identify the amount that is at your disposal for investment purposes. We will discuss the different ways to invest shortly.

In the beginning, you may not be able to accurately categorise all your expenses. One of the ways to stay on top of your expenses is to monitor them as you spend. Maintain a daily journal for the expenses – write down the date, the nature of the expense, the amount, and categorise it. This will help you track your expenses as they happen. It's critical to stay on top of these during the initial days.

Remember, being diligent and disciplined is absolutely critical. It's easier to get complacent and carried away.

Believe me, when I finished doing this exercise, I realised the amount of money that I was spending on silly and unwanted things was significant. When I began cutting down some portion of that, the amount of cash that I was left with grew significantly.

MONEY MATTERS

In the table below, write down the money that you spent during the month.

Date	Expense	Unavoidable	Avoidable	Money-Stealer

Total:

I have spent …..% of my monthly income on "**money-stealers.**"

By cutting down 50% of my **avoidable expenses** and avoiding the **money-stealers**, I can save Rs……….. every month.

3

INSURANCE

I still remember – soon after I got my first job, financial advice started pouring in from all over. The most common advice that I got was to take an insurance policy. Why? Because insurance is needed. It'll help save tax, and it'll give you handsome returns after "X" years that are tax-free. Just like many others, I, along with my brothers and a few friends, went on a rampage and bought policies. The result? The agent who sold the policies was the top agent across the country that year!

Don't get me wrong and think that I'm against insurance policies. Look at the following aspects before buying any insurance policy:

1. **Employer-provided insurance**: These days, most of the companies that we work for, provide insurance – both life and medical. The coverage provided is usually decent. Before you take any policy, see what your employer is providing and assess if it's adequate. If you think it's inadequate, then go for additional insurance. If you think it's adequate, then there's no need for additional insurance. Your insurance needs depend on your financial needs and your health situation.

2. **Insurance to save tax**: Never take policies just because they will help you save tax. Take policies only if you need them.

3. **Insurance for investment**: This is a trap that most of us fall into. We fall for the sales pitch that talks about a particular policy giving us XX lakhs after YY years.

Remember, take insurance only when you feel that there is a need. I don't mean to say that you should take medical insurance after you fall sick. What I mean is that you should opt for an insurance cover either when you don't have any cover, or you feel that the cover you have is insufficient. For this, you need to assess your financials from time to time.

If you need to take additional life insurance, I always suggest you go for a term life plan and not a whole life plan. A term life plan comes at a fraction of the cost compared to that of a whole life plan and the premium saved can be invested in the market for better returns.

One way could be to take a policy and top it up periodically. Say you're 23. If you buy a term life plan for a cover of Rs. 1 crore, the premium that you pay will be around Rs. 10000 a year. As you progress in life, you can increase the cover. The savings in the premium can be diligently invested for better returns.

While people may argue that the returns from insurance are tax-free, my recommendation is that if you invest wisely, your returns after tax would still be a lot better than what you get from an insurance policy.

Once I realised it, I closed all the policies and took one term life policy. I saved over Rs. 15k a month and got an increased life cover.

5

CAR

Traditionally, Indians always had three basic needs – *roti, kapda, aur makaan (food, clothes, and shelter)*. A fourth one got added to these three. No, I'm not referring to the Internet or smartphones. I'm talking about a vehicle. These days, with the geographical distances increasing, a vehicle has become a basic need.

I bought my first car within a few months of getting my first job. As my career progressed, my car kept growing, both in terms of its size and cost. The car became more of an ego booster than a necessity.

Historically, the surge in transportation needs resulted in a serious mismatch in the demand and supply equation. The transport authorities could not aggressively meet their customer needs. The crumbling infrastructure wasn't helping either. The period from 1990 to almost 2015 can be categorised as a transit phase where we saw a tremendous rise in transportation needs. In almost all cities across India, the city buses were irregular, and the metro/taxis/local trains were as good as non-existent. And the auto rickshaws? Let's not talk about them. All these factors were pushing individuals to address their own transport needs. This, along with a surge in disposable income, resulted in a demand for cars.

Since the advent of the 2010s (or a little before), the authorities recognised this need. They began making road transport more dependable and started building metro trains.

The private entrepreneurs chipped in with their share of contribution by coming up with app-based taxis, carpool rides, and self-driving cars on rent. All these began reducing the dependence on private transport.

However, I must say that we are a bit slow in realising that fact. We continue to think that having a car is a basic need. With so many options available, you really don't need to own a car.

OWN CAR VS. CAB

Let's do a detailed comparison between the cost of owning a car and a cab. The numbers below are approximate and based on following assumptions:

Cost of the Car	Rs. 6,50,000
Re-sale value @ 5years	Rs. 2,50,000
Loan Amount	Rs. 5,00,000
Interest rate & Tenure	9% per year and 5 years
Interest paid in 5 years	Rs. 1,23,000
Insurance	Rs. 9,000/year
Maintenance	Rs. 12,000/year
Cost of an app-based taxi	Rs. 13/km (peak rate)
Distance/month	1000 km
Mileage & fuel rate	18km/L and Rs. 75/L

Ownership Cost (monthly)		Cab Charges	
Interest[1]	Rs. 2,050		
Insurance	Rs. 750	Distance	1000 km
Maintenance	Rs. 1,000	Cost/km[2]	Rs. 13

MONEY MATTERS

List down the details of the outstanding loans that you have till now or the loans that you plan to take in the table below.

Loan type	Principle	Annual Interest (%)	Annual Interest (Rs.)	Tenure (years)	Total Interest payable
Total					

Note:

1. If the interest rates are on diminishing balance, then the calculation will not be a straightforward multiplication.

2. The total interest payable shows the amount of your hard-earned money that is taken away by the lender. If you fill in all the lines provided in the table or need more lines, then you're in serious trouble and need help.

6

INVESTMENTS

Till now we mostly spoke about the 'don'ts' in financial planning. Now that you've saved enough money, let's talk about what you should be doing with it:

Before we discuss various investment propositions, you need to keep the following in mind:

1. **Invest surplus**: You probably have heard about some stock market superheroes who took loans, invested them, and made it big. There probably are a handful of such supermen, but you get to hear about their stories a zillion times… Thanks to social media like Whatsapp and Facebook. What you don't often hear is about the numerous instances where people took loans, invested in the market, and were pushed to the brink of disaster or even ended their lives. Remember one thing, always invest surplus cash that is at your disposal. Never make the cardinal mistake of taking a loan to invest.

2. **Risk appetite**: There are multiple definitions around the world for this, and you can easily get one by looking up the web. But in simple terms, it's your ability to cope with the loss of the investments that you make. It's important that you understand your risk appetite as this determines your course of investment.

3. **Tenure**: You're an investor and not a trader. It's always important to remember that you can get healthy returns from the market only when you stay invested.

> It'll take years to build a fortress, but if you managed to build it in a day, then it surely is a sand castle.

Now let's discuss the various investment options (always consult your financial advisor before taking any investment decision).

Firstly, let's speak about bank deposits. Bank deposits (fixed or recurring or any other type) have been the oldest forms of investments known to us. With low-interest rates, the return that these investments give is very less. Added to that, there's a tax liability attached to it. Hence, I do not recommend this to anyone.

The other option that we have in the market is mutual funds. There is a wide range of mutual funds managed by various asset management companies (AMCs) available in the market. There are debt/equity/balanced, open/close ended, sector-specific funds, and various other options available in the market. Choose the type of fund(s) based on your financial needs and risk appetite. The longer you stay invested, the more the benefits.

Let's say that you start working at the age of 22. If you invest Rs. 10k every month for the next 23 years in a mutual fund, your total investment would be Rs. 27.6 lakhs. If that fund generated 10% annual return, you'll have Rs. 1.06 crores in your account, and if that fund generated an annual return of 15% then you'll have Rs. 2.17 crores.

Historically, you can find that certain funds generated 20% or more over a longer tenure. So, if you carefully select the fund to invest, you can get more than 15% return annually. Imagine… Just 10,000 rupees a month giving you over 2 crores. This, along with your retirement benefits, can easily give you the kind of corpus that you are looking for – so retiring at 45 and pursuing your dreams without compromising on your needs isn't wishful thinking anymore.

The last investment option that I would like to discuss is equity or shares or stock. The stocks are categorised as large cap, mid cap, and small cap. When investing in stocks, please seek help from a trusted professional. While mutual funds spread your investment over multiple equities and debt instruments, investing in shares directly will expose you to the risks and rewards that the stock offers. So, tread cautiously!

The other day I saw a news item about a bungalow on Napean Sea Road, Mumbai. It was bought in the year 1917 for Rs. 1 lakh and was sold in the year 2016 for an astronomical amount of Rs. 400 crores. That's a whopping 40,000 times the appreciation! In the year 2001, the shares of MRF Ltd. were trading at Rs. 500/share. The same share was trading at Rs. 50,000 in August 2016… A meagre 100 times. But if you look at the annual return given by each of these assets – the annual return by the piece of land is 11% while the stock delivered over 30% return annually.

If you think this is an outlier, let's look at another company. In their AGM in July 2017, the CEO of Reliance Industries, Mr. Mukesh Ambani, had said that those who invested Rs. 10,000 in 1977 would have seen their investments grow over Rs. 1 crore today – almost 19% return annually. Even some mutual funds would have generated more returns than 11%. While you would have no issues selling the stock and getting paid for it within a couple of days, how many buyers do you think would come forward to buy a piece of land for Rs. 400 crores? You may argue that a piece of land is almost certain to deliver returns but investments in market instruments like mutual funds and stocks are prone to risks. Don't forget that investing in land also comes with its own share of risks. In my opinion, investing in a mutual fund or a stock is far more sensible.

However, I want you to keep the following things in mind while investing in stocks and mutual funds:

1. **Asset Allocation**: Your fund allocation should be based on your risk appetite. In my opinion, a person with a low-risk appetite should allocate the investments to equity and mutual funds in a 10:90 ratio. While a medium risk profile should have it at 25:75 and a high-risk profile should have it at a 50:50 ratio. Such an allocation between equity and mutual funds will not only help you absorb market shocks/volatility but also protect your capital to an extent. If for some reason, you need to withdraw money from the market for use and unfortunately there is a prolonged bloodbath in the market, you will be able to pick the most profitable option to withdraw from. Remember that these are not based on any research but are based on my experience.

2. **Systematic Investment Plan (SIP)**: The best way to invest is by way of a SIP. This will help you by averaging out the cost of investment. Also, it makes investing a habit. Whether equity or mutual funds, there are multiple SIP frequency options that you can choose from.

3. **Periodic Review**: Once you start investing, please ensure that you review your portfolio periodically. You should do this at least once a year. Take professional help if needed. This will help you to assess and correct if needed.

4. **No shortcuts**: Don't fall for the 'multi-bagger' traps. While the multi-baggers stocks sound promising, never ever give them more than 10% of the total amount that you have in your equity portfolio.

So, if you carefully pick your investment vehicle, you will be able to build a very healthy corpus required for your retirement by the age of forty-five (or sooner). This financial independence will help you pursue your dreams or passions without any fear.

While there are many other investment options like the derivatives available in the market, I avoided discussing them here, as my intent is to provide you with options that are safe and reliable. In addition, the options that we discussed do not need you to spend the whole day monitoring them.

So, be diligent while selecting your vehicle as an investment and stay invested to reap benefits. If you follow a balanced and prudent approach, you will certainly accomplish your financial goals... Sooner than you expect.

7

IN A NUTSHELL

1. Categorise your expenses (unavoidable, avoidable, and wasteful) and track them.

2. Before buying insurance, assess your insurance needs and the coverage that you already have – self-funded and employer-provided.

3. Given house property value can't be realised quickly, buy it only when the need is compelling and the EMI is less than 25% of your income.

4. A car is a depreciating asset. Buy it only when there is an absolute need. Remember, the car should serve you… Not your status or ego.

5. Carefully select the investment option (mutual fund or equity) and the fund allocation to each option based on key criteria. If needed, hire a coach to help you chart the path and accomplish the goals.

8

YOUR WAY FORWARD

When needed, you usually seek help from your 'Go-To Folks'. These 'Go-To Folks' are either your family/ friends or your personal banker or a financial planner. While some are certified and experienced, others are not. Some challenges in having them plan your financial goals are:

HOLISTIC APPROACH

They often don't have detailed insights into your life. Their focus is purely on your investments or your present situation. They don't really look into your aspirations and dreams, your goals, your responsibilities and your challenges (both personal and professional). In many instances, changes in your life require you to change your financial plans. Without these insights, the investment plans and the advice that you get from them will be incomplete. Also, their suggestions/advice are often based on that instance.

VESTED INTERESTS

Some (not all) of these financial planners/ advisors have a vested interest – their monthly targets, the brokerage they receive from the investment houses, and so on. As a result, some of the advice that you get may not suit you.

This is where having a coach will help. A coach will work with you in charting the path, monitoring the progress, and helps you stay on course. In addition, the coach will not give you solutions but will make you become self-sufficient to find solutions by yourself.

In many instances, people approach me saying that they need to focus on one aspect of their life – this is usually the tip of the iceberg. But as the coaching sessions progress, I scratch the surface and dug deeper to arrive at a different aspect of life to focus on. This root cause was totally different from what was originally assumed to be the issue. Addressing this will help address other aspects of their lives.

Once a lady approached me and said that she needs to reduce weight, be more active, and exercise regularly. As we began the coaching sessions, it turned out that she first needed to make changes to her daily schedule at work. While this was completely different from what she thought was the problem, she realised that this would help her address many other issues.

While a coach doesn't come free, those who sought the help of the right coach would agree that it's an investment that is worth making.

Remember, a professional coach will never divulge your personal details – your details are safe and confidential. This will help you speak to your coach in full confidence.

LIFE AHEAD

In the table below, list down three key tasks that you will be doing and monitor them regularly.

You will write down what exactly you would do to improve your financial situation, by when will you do this (mention a clear date or a month), and how this will help you.

What	When	Impact

Once you list down your takeaways in the table below, against each takeaway, mention how you will measure if the takeaway listed above is completed or not. Remember, if you are unable to measure its success, it probably means that it wasn't defined properly.

What	Measure of Success

Dream...Believe...Achieve!